Greetings from Kenyon

by

John L. Cole

An aerial view of Kenyon, Minnesota taken in the early 1930s. *Post card by James Rueber*

ISBN: 0-9676652-0-5

Printed November, 1999

Layout & Design by
Noah Publishing, Inc.
638 2nd St.
Kenyon, MN 55946

INTRODUCTION

This book contains a 25-year collection of Kenyon post cards. Most of the cards were bought at post card shows, flea markets, antique malls, and through the mail from other collectors. Some of the cards were given to me by people who heard that I collected Kenyon cards. I recorded their names on the back of each card I was given, but they are not listed in the book as I might forget someone and wouldn't want to do that. When people found out that I collected Kenyon post cards, the price of those cards went sky-high. I never turned down a card I didn't have regardless of the price. Some cards only become available once, and then it's now or never.

It was fun collecting and in the process I met a lot of nice people. Some were very helpful in helping me identify objects on the cards. Some years ago, I showed my cards at the Carriage and Cutter Parade in the vacant Self-Serve Grocery building. I was just about to take down my display when Alice Held came in. She wanted to see my cards and for the next two hours we sat and chatted about each card. This lady is a walking "Kenyon History Book." As we looked at each card, she told me things I did not know about our town. I received a lot of knowledge that day and will be forever grateful for the chance we had. A few days later she sent me a letter thanking me for letting her see the cards. She also enclosed a post card of her home with a picture of her mother and a neighbor on it. She said if I didn't want the card to give it to her nephew Howard. I want you to know that Howard didn't get it. Sorry Howard.

Through the years my collection grew to over 350 picture post cards and to over 125 greeting and advertising cards. What would a collection of this be worth? I have no idea, probably priceless. Once this collection is broken up it cannot be replaced and that's why I chose to do this book. I had thought about doing the cards on video cassette but with today's technology it would end up like the stereo cards of the 1900s. A book seemed the only way to go. A book did not require any special equipment. A book could be picked up and put down without special programming and it didn't have to be rewound.

I had worked with the *Kenyon Leader* when the All-School Reunion book was put out and I liked their work. Doug Noah is a very nice person to work with. We used over 200 post cards, and some may be the same subject but from a different angle adding to more background information. What I tried to do was give as much information as to what Kenyon looked like as the town changed. I borrowed cards from some other collections and their names are listed below the cards I used. There are still a lot of cards to be found. I have provided a couple of pages in the back and if you wish, you can put your own post cards there.

I hope you enjoy the book as much as I did collecting the cards. I had one post card made of Main Street a few years ago but other than that all the cards were made by some very talented photographers. Local photographers took most of the pictures in the Golden Age of post cards which was from 1900 to 1930. After that there were only a couple of firms that came around and took pictures for cards until the 1960s.

<u>Post cards for this book were made by the following:</u>

- J.T. Austinson
- M.W. Wright
- O. Steihaug
- Borlaug
- Lainson
- A. Pearson
- CO MO CO
- L.L. Cook
- The Smiths
- Big 4 Post Card Co.
- Johnson & Olson

And lots of unknowns

Without their help, this book could not have been made.

<u>THIS BOOK IS DEDICATED TO:</u>

•My Great-Grandfather, John A. Hansen, owner Leuthold & Hansen, 1885 to 1924

•My grandfather, Orlando C. Cole, owner and publisher of The Kenyon Leader, 1910 to 1950

•My father, John S. Cole, postal clerk, postmaster, 1958 to 1961

•My wife of many wonderful years, Lila Mae

•My children, Lynn, Wendy, Sherry and Dean

•My grandchildren, Scott, Christine, Kelly, Heather, Heidi, Cory and Noah

It is good to remember the past but always look to the future.

ABOUT KENYON

The Village is:

Kenyon, Minnesota 55946

Located in:

The southwest corner of Goodhue County

Named after:

Kenyon College in Gambier, Ohio

Village platted by:

James M. LeDuc (Kenyon College graduate)

James H. Day

Byron C. Howe

Addison Holton

Incorporated as Village:

First elections for village officers were held in 1885

Earliest post card. Building in front of two elevators on left is Commercial House Hotel built as American House in 1885. Smoke coming from Gunderson generating plant. Buildings in front to right are Main Street businesses (unknown) except farthest one east is Lohmans City Livery Stable. Streets are dirt.

Early view of Kenyon Public School dated 1906. This school was located on Forest Street in the same spot as 1916 Grade and High School.

•1907•

Prior to this date, post cards could only have address on one side with writing done around pictures on other side.

The brick Hommedahl building built in 1885. The sign in the window of far right building says "The Corner Bar". This building and seven more to the left were destroyed by fire in 1908.

The Stene building built in 1895 now is the VFW Post Home. Buildings from right to left: (1) U.S. Post Office. Sign on the back door of Post Office says "The News"; (2) Aaker Grocery, (3) Brobeck Drug recently purchased from C.O. Heyerdahl; (4) unknown.

•1968•

Roseview Apartments built for $132,000 from F.H.A.

Members of the Minnesota National Guard pictured on horse back on their way to camp Lake View in Lake City, Minnesota. The State Militia spent 10 days at camp each year and came through Kenyon from cities to the west. They pulled supply wagons and cannons. Circa 1906-1911.

Kenyon Main Street after 1912. The Lyric Theater on left was the first picture show in town and the early movies had no sound, but subtitles were displayed on screen. Someone usually played a piano to the story on the screen. The Central Hotel sign was not painted on that building until 1912.

•1907•
Steel water tower built on hill next to Red Wing Avenue

The back of this card says "Taken at George Elcock residence (110 Gunderson Blvd.) at a Valentine party February 14, 1913." This is what a living room was like at that time.

It wasn't unusual to take a picture of uncle Charles in his coffin and have it put on post card paper so it could be sent to relatives in North Dakota who couldn't come to the funeral so they could see "how nice he looked." This card is a funeral floral display.

•1964•
Voters reject building a municipal building.

The German Evangelical Church was built around 1914. Fourth Street doesn't even appear - just a sidewalk.

The same church all by itself with only building of the Milwaukee Railroad in background to right. *Post card by Gladys Mund*

•1980•
Milwaukee Railroad line east and west through Kenyon abandoned.

A winter day on Main Street. Note runners on wagons. Most wagons could be changed from wheels to runners. Circa 1906-1912.

North side of Main Street looking from Forest Street. Classen Opera House pictured in middle of photo.

•1915•
Central Hotel and Restaurant served Kenyon Kvality Kream, the best ice cream with pure fruit flavor

Private mailing card, circa 1900-1907. Mogren Hill pictured on the right. House was destroyed by fire in 1997.

Main Street buildings after fire. A vacant lot existed between fourth and sixth building. Lewis Wenzel Harness shop filled the space in 1910 or 1911.

•1958•
Village approved a resolution to purchase the Time Theater building for $18,500 for a Municipal Liquor dispensary.

The April 1, 1908 fire started in the middle of Main Street and strong winds drove the fire east to the end of the block. Buildings could have been saved, but firefighters ran out of water.

Both fire pictures were taken from the corner of Red Wing Ave and Second Street looking west. The two young men pictured are, from left, William Golden and Gilman Satron. The pile of bricks on the left is what remained of the Hommedal building.

•1974•
Closest mayoral race in history of Kenyon. Councilman John Cole unseated Mayor Clarence Dahlen by a six vote margin 307 to 301.

State Militia heading to camp at Lake City. The center of the picture shows the group pulling a cannon. All the buildings to the right of the P.L. Berg Dry Goods store were destroyed in the April Fools Day fire of 1908.

North side of Main Street sometime after 1912 - note horse hitching rails in street by sidewalk. Main Street was dirt - note concrete sidewalk for pedestrian to cross to other side. Street lights shown in the picture were used between 1915 and 1924.

•1989•

First mandatory recycling pickup by Sampson of Waseca, Minnesota

Kenyon's famous stone arch over the Zumbro River. In this spot, a timber bridge was built across the river in 1885 for the Chicago and Northwestern Railroad. The timber bridge was filled in in 1906 by the Chicago Great Western Railroad and was wide enough for two tracks. Cows and the peaceful Zumbro Valley are pictured looking east.

Kenyon's Main Street looking east from Spring Street circa 1910. This set of numbered cards by Johnson and Olson of Alexandria, Minnesota contains at least 18 cards all of which have not been found.

•1974•

Pattridge Hardware building located on the northwest corner of Second Street and Spring Street was reduced to a pile of rubble.

Zumbro River from railroad overpass. The house to the right of the windmill in center of picture is Kermit Flom's house, 506 Front Street. The right side of the river is pasture land.

North Spring Street also known as Lover's Lane. This sidewalk went down the hill where a swing bridge to Trondheim was built. The house is just north of 28 Spring Street and is now a vacant lot. The house was torn down by Dr. Richard Overby.

•1924•

Main Street (Second Street) was poured with concrete for the first time.

All buildings on the south side of Main Street have been removed to make room for modern buildings or Highway 56 from the south. The steam in the picture is from the pump in the city's well house. The church steeple to the left is First Lutheran Church before fire, and elevator on far left is on Milwaukee Railroad line. The Standard Oil corner is nothing but trees and a vacant lot.

The sign over Main Street says "Baseball Sunday". There is still an open spot where Dick's Barbershop is now located (642 2nd St.) on north side of street, and trees were located on south side of street.

•1958•
Fourth annual Kenyon Horse shows held at the Ed Baker farm one mile south of County Road 12.

The building to the far right is the only picture of the Kenyon House built by Swan Selane in 1885. There was a livery large enough for 100 horses. Sometime after 1915 the hotel was cut in half and moved, with half going to 304 4th Street and the other half to 430 3rd Street. This space is now the site of the Cenex Co-op Station.

Three box cars and one gondola on Chicago Great Western siding. Steel bridge on right and wooden tressel belong to Milwaukee Railroad. The square frame on tracks behind telephone pole has leather straps hanging from top bar to let trainmen riding on the top know that a bridge is approaching which could knock them off the train.

•1918•

Because of fuel shortages, Kenyon stores had heatless Mondays

Kenyon Public School building. The center section with tower was built in 1881, the south wing was built in 1897 and the north wing was added in 1902. When the school was razed in 1915 the north wing was moved to Main Street and became the new Kenyon Hotel run by James Feeley.

Residence on right is the George Benson Home, 504 Forest, now occupied by Cornell Lee. The Brusletten House, center, at 512 Forest is now occupied by Julie Farmer.

•1998•
Noon whistle stopped blowing.

Looking east at Wagon Bridge over Zumbro River on north road out of Kenyon. Bridge is still standing today but not used.

Bridge on east Second St. over Pearl Creek. Before Highway 60 was built, this was main road between Kenyon and Wanamingo.

•1998•
Kenyon Police Department taken over by Goodhue County Sheriff's Dept.

The Methodist Church built in 1888 on the southwest corner of Forest and Third on land donated by the Bullis family. House to the left is 322 Forest owned by Greg Amundson.

The same church in 1920s being raised so a basement can be put under it. House under construction on left is 314 Forest St. owned by Herbert Houglum.

•1950•

In local election, the President position has been changed to Mayor by law.

The Methodist Church as it appeared in the 1950s. Services were moved to a larger church in the 60s and this church was torn down in 1970. The church to the right is only photo of St. Matthews German Evangelical Church. Around 1955, this church was used as a temporary ag classroom by Kenyon school system and was torn down in the 1960s.

The Methodists ended up in this church at 429-4th St.

•1942•

Goodhue Canning Co. uses German P.O.W.s (Prisoners of War) as part of their labor force.

The Kenyon Leader and Finstuen Law Office circa 1910. Pictured left to right are, 1 - Oscar Monson (small boy) who ended up working at the Leader his entire life; 2 - O.C. Cole, Jr. - owner; 3 - Chris Sorteberg who ran a land agency in lobby of Kenyon Leader; 4 - Chris Sorteberg's son; 5 - unidentified.

Kenyon City Livery Stable operated by F.F. Lohman from 1904 to 1918. Located on east Main Street where Veterans Park is now located. Building in left background is Kenyon Egg and Poultry Co., taken around 1910. George Lee is pictured on the left holding horse, and Ferdinand F. Lohman is holding horse on the right.

•1895•

Prof. U. Curtis, former owner of The Kenyon Leader opened Lake City Commercial College and English training school

Years ago when film was taken in to be developed, you could specify regular pictures or post card backs. Many one-of-a-kind cards ended up this way. This unidentified man leaning on shovel with Episcopal Church in background is on the corner of Huseth and Second Street.

This picture, mailed in 1909, says "In the party taking in the Fair are, left to right: Ole Gunhus, J.F. Grose, B.F. Grose, Oli Naeseth, Conrad Grose, Henry Sathrum."

•1925•
Kenyon Ventilating Co. launched as a barn roof air circulator manufacturer.

This is a set of at least 10 cards put out by the Big 4 Postcard Co. in about 1914. The picture was taken standing in the center of Main Street and Red Wing Ave. looking west. The first store on the left is Central Garage with an auto repair sign in window. The barn ventilator on right similar to those made by Kenyon Ventilator Co.

There is a sulky (two wheel cart) and, for the first time, two automobiles on the street. Building on right is Golden Rule (variety store) and the garage on the left sold Case Equipment.

•1918•

Sommers Canning Co. was paying $16 per ton for Crosby sweet corn delivered.

Forest and Main Street looking east. The covered buggy in front of bank had "Quality Ice Cream" printed on the side.

Main Street looking west from Forest Street, circa 1915. Gunderson Hardware Store on right is selling barn cupolas located on sidewalk. Streets are dirt.

•1969•
Plymold Booths purchased and became the mainstay of Foldcraft Co.

Red Wing Ave. looking north from water tower. First houses built in that area were in 1907. House on the left: 602 Red Wing Ave (now occupied by Ralph Hagberg). The three houses on east side of road are, from left: 529 Red Wing Ave (Mrs. Merlin Klahr), 535 Red Wing Ave. (Robert Haller), 543 Red Wing Ave. (Frank Huberty).

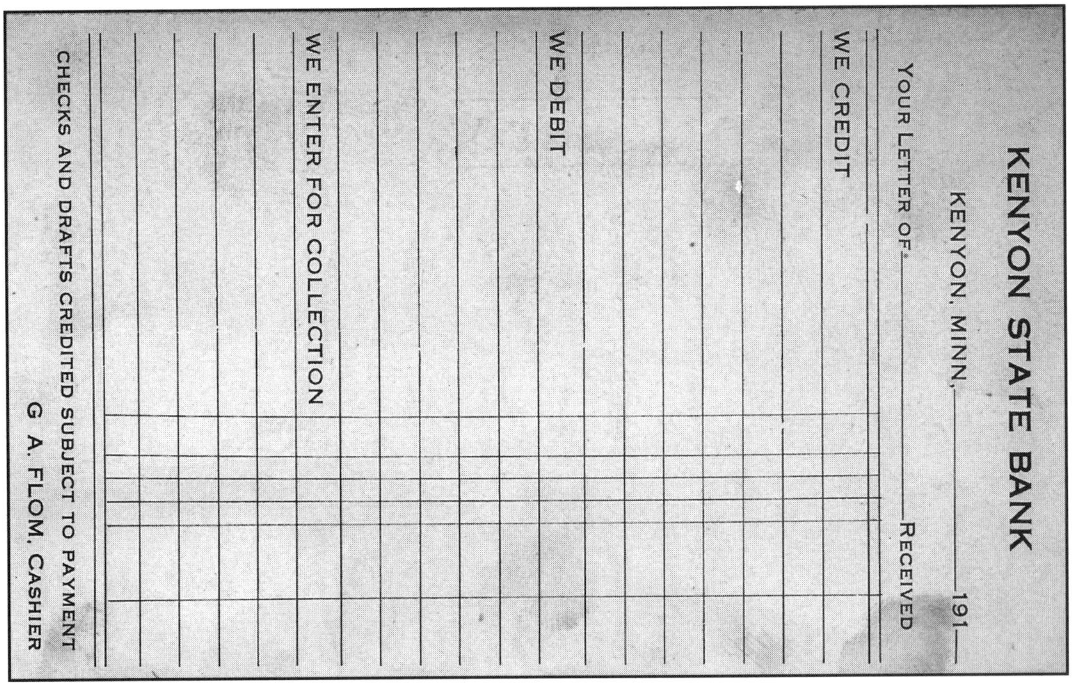

KENYON STATE BANK

KENYON, MINN. ______ 191__

YOUR LETTER OF ______ RECEIVED

WE CREDIT

WE DEBIT

WE ENTER FOR COLLECTION

CHECKS AND DRAFTS CREDITED SUBJECT TO PAYMENT

G. A. FLOM, CASHIER

The Kenyon State Bank used penny postal to transact business. Not a very private way to do bank transactions, but was low cost.

•1930•

Central Hotel and Cafe had 15 bedrooms and one sitting room.

A multi-view post card from around 1912 mailed in Skyberg, Minnesota. Center picture: Episcopal Church; Top right: Sign on Main Street says "market day"; Bottom right: Stene building on Main and Forest; Bottom left: Farmers State Bank and City Hall; Top left: Main Street looking west from Red Wing Ave.

Looking down Mogren Hill from the top. This was the main road into Kenyon from the north. The house to the far right is the Mogren residence and the sidewalk was for Trondheim residents that had to walk to town.

•1993•
GTE started first digital switching equipment.

Built in 1876 by the Episcopalians, this church is called Church of the Ascension and was located on the southeast corner of Gunderson Boulevard and State Street. The writer of this card sent in 1915 says, "the church has no Sunday School so will go to Lutheran Church." Bell tower was originally to be put on roof but moved to above entrance.

The Episcopal property at Kenyon, Minn.

Taken around 1911. Left to right: 1) Guild Hall moved to 121 Third St.; 2) the parsonage is still a home at 209 Gunderson Blvd owned by Mildred Lair; 3) Church of the Ascension.

•1899•

Round Table Club organized by 13 members.

Another view from across the street. Note that the road is a single street and not a divided highway as it is today.

In 1964, Kenyon's oldest church was moved to Faribault to the former St. James school. A duplex is now on the corner where the church stood (203 State St.).

•1866•
One room school house built on southwest corner of Spring and First St.

In the top greeting post card a small envelope attached to the front of the card gave the sender a place to send a personal message. On the lower card the use of verse was very popular and found on many post cards.

•1955•
Kenyon Swimming Pool construction for $80,000

View looking southwest from egg and poultry building at Lawn Street and Langford Ave. Kenyon water tower at left and Kenyon High School at right in background. The house lower left is where Farm and Home now stands. Circa 1913.

This card was made before the 1908 fire. Businesses pictured left to right, are: Citizens State Bank, Nelson Mercantile, Leuthold and Hanson - Kenyon Clothing Co., C.L. Brusletten & Co., H.E. Berg's Central Cafe, Picha Shoes and Eagle Drug in Opera House.

•1870•
Kerosene lights installed on Main Street

Winter time on Main Street. This was the only way to get to town as most country roads were not plowed. It also meant people had to watch where they stepped when crossing the street.

A busy winter day at the Elevator. Farm wagons were filled with sacks of corn or grain to sell or grind. Kenyon Lumber Co. office and storage shed is pictured in the background. This structure was destroyed by a disastrous fire in 1967.

•1904•
Kenyon Commercial Club organized.

The original F.G. Held building located in the same spot as the present day garage. Horse watering fountains were located in the street. The Helds have been on Main Street since 1894.

Founded in 1892 and located one door east of Citizens State Bank, Nelson Mercantile remained in business until the late 1920s. J.C.E. Holman bought out Harold Nelson in the early 1900s. *Post card by Howard Held*

•1929•
Kenyon Golf Club organized.

Pattridge Hardware Store on the northwest corner of Spring and Main operated from 1890 to 1942. Building was torn down in 1974. *Post card by Robert Peterson*

Believed to be the interior of Pattridge Hardware. Inside picture post cards of stores are in great demand and are hard to find. *Post card by Robert Peterson*

•1890•

Mogren Ice House cut 300 ton of ice from Zumbro River.

Not every day was Market Day but when it was a sign was hung over Main Street. It was a busy day in Kenyon as many buggies and one automobile are pictured. *Post card by Howard Held*

Jay Held pictured standing across the street from the following businesses, right to left: Pattridge Hardware, unknown, unknown, but purchased by Frank Held and moved to left 50 feet and made into a house (424 Gunderson Blvd.) now owned by Steve Nesseth. *Post card by Howard Held*

•1996•
North Star Creamery and 128' brick smoke stack torn down.

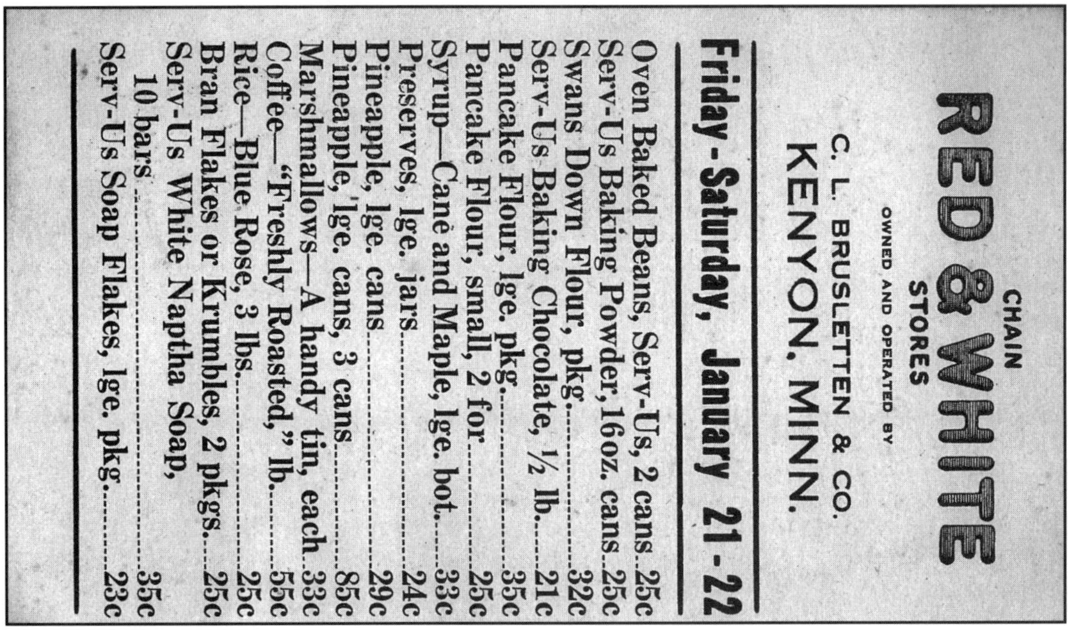

CHAIN
RED & WHITE
STORES
OWNED AND OPERATED BY
C. L. BRUSLETTEN & CO.
KENYON, MINN.

Friday-Saturday, January 21-22

Oven Baked Beans, Serv-Us, 2 cans	25c
Serv-Us Baking Powder, 16oz. cans	25c
Swans Down Flour, pkg.	32c
Serv-Us Baking Chocolate, ½ lb.	21c
Pancake Flour, lge. pkg.	35c
Pancake Flour, small, 2 for	25c
Syrup—Cane and Maple, lge. bot.	33c
Preserves, lge. jars	24c
Pineapple, lge. cans	29c
Pineapple, lge. cans, 3 cans	85c
Marshmallows—A handy tin, each	33c
Coffee—"Freshly Roasted," lb.	55c
Rice—Blue Rose, 3 lbs.	25c
Bran Flakes or Krumbles, 2 pkgs.	25c
Serv-Us White Naptha Soap, 10 bars	35c
Serv-Us Soap Flakes, lge. pkg.	23c

Grocery shoppers could fine bargains as this 1927 ad from the Red and White store shows. C.L. Brusletten started out in 1879 on Main Street between Spring and Bullis on the south side of the street. *Post card by Robert Peterson*

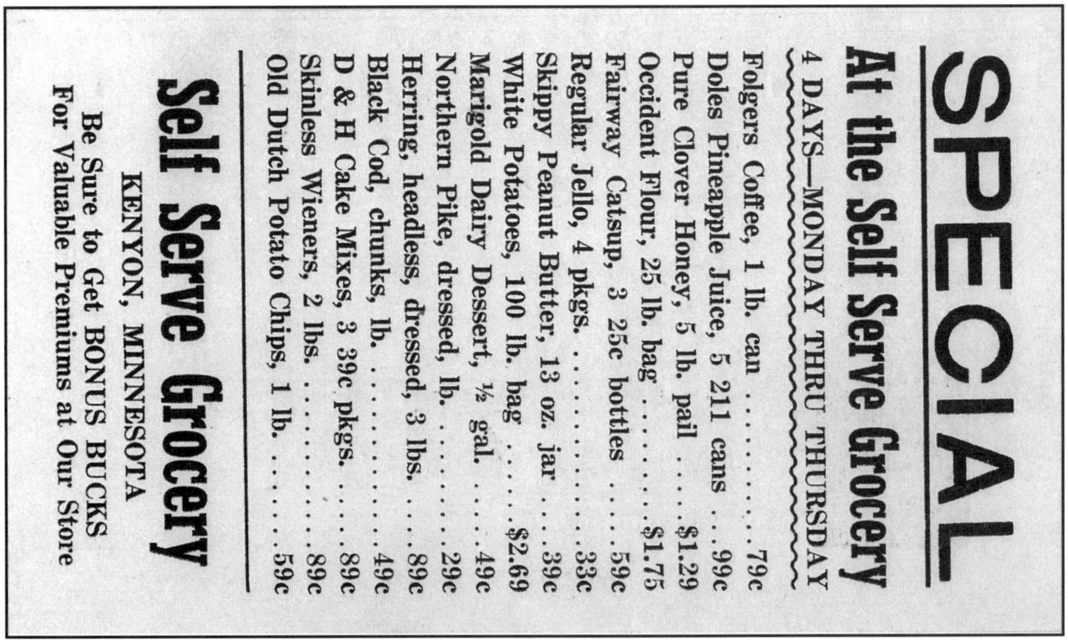

SPECIAL
At the Self Serve Grocery
4 DAYS—MONDAY THRU THURSDAY

Folgers Coffee, 1 lb. can	79c
Doles Pineapple Juice, 5 211 cans	99c
Pure Clover Honey, 5 lb. pail	$1.29
Occident Flour, 25 lb. bag	$1.75
Fairway Catsup, 3 25c bottles	59c
Regular Jello, 4 pkgs.	33c
Skippy Peanut Butter, 13 oz. jar	39c
White Potatoes, 100 lb. bag	$2.69
Marigold Dairy Dessert, ½ gal.	49c
Northern Pike, dressed, lb.	29c
Herring, headless, dressed, 3 lbs.	89c
Black Cod, chunks, lb.	49c
D & H Cake Mixes, 3 39c pkgs.	89c
Skinless Wieners, 2 lbs.	89c
Old Dutch Potato Chips, 1 lb.	59c

Self Serve Grocery
KENYON, MINNESOTA
Be Sure to Get BONUS BUCKS
For Valuable Premiums at Our Store

This 1958 ad from Self Serve Grocery came out one year before Pete Dyrdahl and Archie Kramer sold their store having been in business since 1925.

•1918•

Thorstein Skarning, world's greatest accordian player, appeared and played at Kenyon High School.

The I.O.O.F. building with the hardware store on the left half. Tornblad and Pederson ran it from 1908-1912 and Albert Hilstad and Ole Pederson from 1912-1919. Right half is vacant. *Post card by Gladys Mund*

Card mailed in 1908 of VFW building with Post Office located on corner. Wood frame buildings to the left have been removed and replaced with brick structures. Unsure of the owners during this time.

•1891•
Iron bridge built across Zumbro River by Luebke Bros.
and is still standing but not used.

Looking north across Zumbro River at Trondheim road. Houses, left to right: 118 Trondheim Road (now occupied by Bob Boesen); Luebke Bros. (106 Trondheim Road), now owned by Brad Luebke (grand nephew); Sweede Callen house moved to 310 4th St.

Man standing on Pearl Creek bridge. House and barn is Luebke Bros. (106 Trondheim Rd.). Spring of the year as river is up. In 1890 Luebke Bros. ran a hotel here as this was main road north out of Kenyon.

•1993•

Clothing Doc in Opera House and Coast to Coast were torn down to make room for new Security State Bank building.

Looking west at arch. Stream to left coming from Chicago Great Western pump house used to fill water tank on Main Street which in turn filled the steam trains.

There are about two dozen cards taken of the Zumbro River. Most show the stone arch or cows grazing.

•1897•
Population of Village of Kenyon was 1635.

Starting out southwest of Kenyon in a little stone church, the Hauge Lutheran congregation moved into a new frame church in Kenyon in 1903. First house to the left is 322 4th Street, second house is 406 Bullis, third house is 412 Bullis, and fourth house is roof of Milwaukee Depot.

The church as it looks today. The parsonage to the right was built in 1953. A new weather proof entrance was built in 1964.

•1887•
Volunteer fire department starts with 40 members.

Hauge's choir, circa 1907. This was a post card with a Christmas wish on the back.

The original church parsonage at 506 Front Street built around 1890. Now the home of Kermit Flom. *Post card by Howard Held*

•1903•
Kenyon Canning Co. organized.

Farmers State Bank built in 1903 by B.J. Borlaug, who may be the person standing in the doorway. Building in left background is only view of the Blacksmith shop.

A few years later, the front of the building next to the bank was changed to look like the bank to give the impression of one building. City Hall and fire department are pictured to the right. Circa 1917.

•1901•

Kenyon Telephone Company started by Dr. Gates.

This is from a set of 16 cards by an unknown photographer. Believed to be 1918 Memorial Day parade.

•1913•
Carren Brothers road show appeared at Opera House.

Nelson Mercantile Co. operated from 1892 to the late 1920s. Their store was the first place east of Citizens State Bank. This was a good price for a coat at that time.

POULTRY CAR AT KENYON

Tuesday, Aug. 12th, 1919

We'll have a Poultry Car stop at Kenyon every Tuesday up to the end of the season Our first poultry car will stop here Tuesday, Aug. 12th. Bring your poultry in for this car and get the following prices in cash:

Hens - - -	**24 cents**
Springs - - -	**28 cents**
Roosters - - -	**13 cents**
Ducks - - -	**20 cents**
Geese - - -	**13 cents**

Pigeons, $1 per dozen.

Higher prices will be paid on day of delivery if market warrants.

Aug. Johnston, Manager.
Hammer's Cream Station

Bring your eggs along and get cash for them.

The railroad had special cars built for transporting chickens which eventually ended at a poultry processing plant. August Johnston was the local constable for many years.

•1913•
Kenyon Leader was published on Saturdays

A flag pole in Main Street!!! Taken in the early 1920s, the flag pole may have been used at Dr. Gates' funeral as it shows up there only. Balcony on VFW was used by photographers to shoot parade pictures.

Charles Harrison Funeral Parlor and Furniture Store is located on the right in the IOOF building. The third building from left with arched doorway is the Lyric Theater.

•1885•
Kenyon was incorporated as a village.

One of the first post cards of the new concrete pavement laid on Main Street in 1924. No more mud, a lot more automobiles and still one horse.

Kenyon's boulevard looking east from Huseth Street. The church on the right is Church of the Ascension Episcopal which was moved to Faribault. Circa 1930s.

•1930•
Lyric Theater installed sound film equipment

Buildings pictured left to right, are: Opera House with E.O. Bakko downstairs advertising silverware on awning; Sands Brothers Grocery; Lunds Clothing House; unknown; Porter Dry Cleaning; P.L. Berg Dry Goods Store; Central Hotel & Cafe.

The Citizen State Bank built in 1915. This picture was taken in the late 1920s as Self Serve Grocery opened for business in 1928.

•1959•

City-wide mail delivery started by Postmaster Cole

In my collection, I have over 100 different Greeting from Kenyon cards. The word Kenyon is either printed, stamped or written.

Metal add-ons (two hands) were very popular at one time. You could find horseshoes, cars, deer, and flowers attached to the card.

•1986•
The new water tower had a rose painted on it.

View of the North Star Creamery just after it was built in 1920. The lot to the right has rolls of wire fencing and cattle watering tanks.

North Star Creamery with power house and smoke stack on the right. Note store building to the left.

•1919•
Kenyon Boy Scouts organized.

Largest funeral in Kenyon, with 4,000 people attending services held for Dr. Joseph A. Gates who was killed one mile south of town after his car was hit by a train June 19, 1922. *Post card by Mabel Gates*

The band and a group of soldiers and sailors make up one of the first groups. There is a set of 12 cards that show the complete seven block procession that made its way down Kenyon's Main Street.

•1938•
Kenyon Frozen Food Locker plant opened with lockers for rent.

Eastern Star members pictured carrying wreaths. Note the flag pole in the center of the street.

A group of Knight Templar, Masons, professional and political people pay their respects by marching to the cemetery. A special train on the Chicago Great Western line brought many mourners from the Twin Cities.

•1896•
Electric Generating Plant started by M.T. Gunderson

The hearse carrying Dr. Gates followed by a motorcade of family members and friends.

Hearse with honor guard arrives at Kenyon City Cemetery for committal services. Services were held at the Gates residence 27 Spring St. on the lawn as there wasn't a church large enough to hold everyone who came.

•1907•

Village set speed limit at eight miles per hour so not to scare horses.

Some of the many floral displays that covered the cemetery grounds.

After the ceremony at the cemetery the mourners returned to the Gates home. Here is the band and fraternal groups marching north on Spring Street.

•1923•

West End tourist park leased for five years with option to buy.

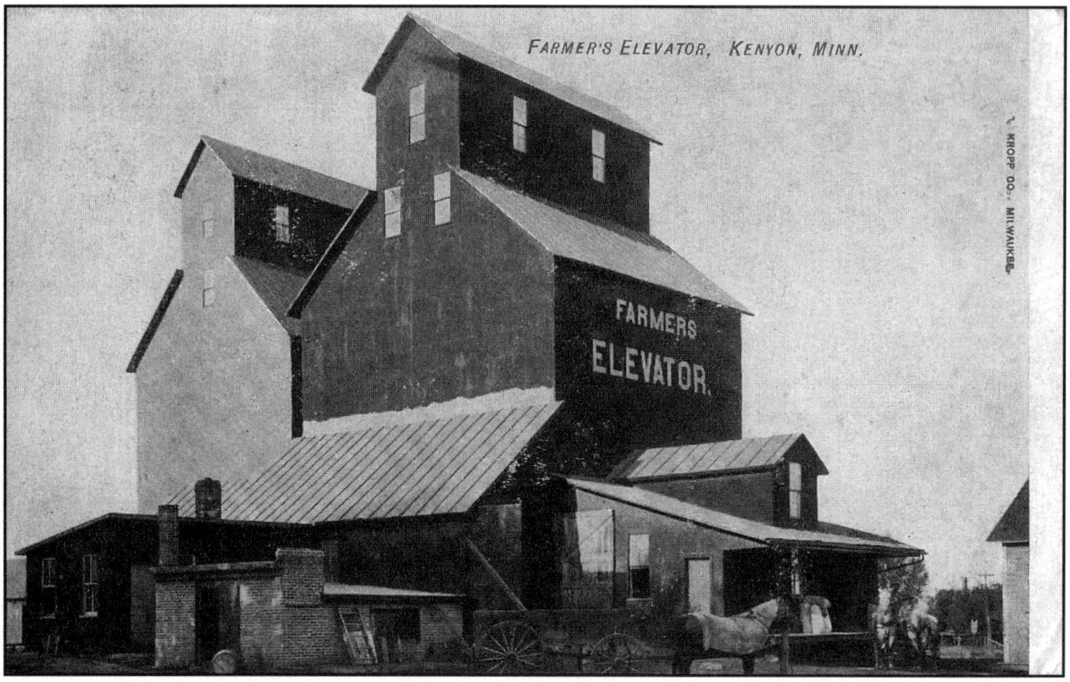

Post marked 1908, this picture shows the earliest elevator post card. Built in 1895 as a co-op, it lasted 100 years and was finally taken over by Cannon Valley Co-op.

1930s card of the elevator. Note there is an auto with trailer and a horse and buggy with a milk can in back. Both are getting supplies. New office has been built. There is nothing left of this complex today.

•1946•

Vets housing with 20 units built on Fourth and State.

Late 1930s. Truck on left sitting on scale next to bins where homeowners could get coal for their home and have it weighed. New center building for feed grinding and mixing.

Farmers Implement built in 1936. Started here in 1913 and stayed here until 1974 when space forced it to move north of town.

•1928•

North Star Ginseng Garden started to supply ginseng for Chinese medicine.

World War I produced a lot of one-of-a-kind post cards. This one is of Nels Wangsness at camp in front of his tent.

The Kenyon VFW is named after one of the first Goodhue County soldiers to be killed in the war. Pictured left to right is: Conrad Osthum (who the VFW is named after), Ben Danielson, Nels Wangsness, Peter Semb. Boy standing in front is James Danielson.

•1938•
First air mail pick-up from Kenyon.

Lenard Stremback, Sogn cheesemaker, is very proud of the deer he shot near Mora, MN in 1917 on this card sent to Halvor Lillesve.

This card, sent in 1911, said on the back, "Glad it finally rained as cistern was getting very low." Pictured left to right is horse, J.H.B., Casper Gilles, and Herman Bauer.

•1957•
Kenyon Development Corp. incorporated.

An early photo of Vang Church by J.T. Austinson, local photographer and post card maker. He is buried in Vang Cemetery.

Early photo (date unknown) of the inside of Vang Church. The minister (with white collar) is standing behind a confirmation class.

•1935•
Village Council accepted the library as Village property, and assumed its proper support under state library laws.

The church as it looked in the 1970s. This church, built in 1895, was built one mile north of first church that was erected in 1863.

A beautiful view of the inside of Vang Church showing organ pipes. Inside views are very hard to find. J.T. Austinson took this one from balcony. Note hanging gas lamp in lower center.

•1935•

There were seven churches, Episcopal, Methodist, Norwegian Lutheran, German Lutheran, Hauge Lutheran, Bethany Lutheran, and German Evangelical.

Built on Forest Street, this is Kenyon's first brick school. Center section with tower was built in 1889. In 1897, the right wing was added. In 1902, the north wing was built with a gymnasium in the basement.

This card, written in 1913 in German and sent to West Concord to Gjory Aase, shows a group of school children outside center tower of school.

•1959•

Blacksmith shop built at the turn of the century was torn down to make room for Dr. Jacobson's dental office.

Milwaukee track in foreground looking north from Forest St. This 1908 photo shows school children playing, climbing poles, etc., in school yard. Note coaster wagon lower right.

Post marked 1908. Girl in white, #13 from left in back row, is Harriet Wegner. Little girl to her right, #12, is Francis (Fanny) Wegner or Mrs. Harry Bergh, wife of drug store owner.

•1990•

Kenyon school paired with Wanamingo and combined in 1993.

Kenyon Grade and High School built in the same spot as the old school in 1916. Raised concrete to block in foreground is a buggy step with hitching post to left. The dirt road is Forest Street.

In 1938, a new auditorium and gymnasium was added to the north of the original 1916 structure.

•1885•
First Kenyon Leader published.

In 1954 an elementary school was built on 10 acres of land the school had purchased in 1942 for playground and sports complex. Located north of Sixth Street and west of Spring Street.

In 1962 a new gynasium was built on land purchased to the north. Thirteen new classrooms and administrative offices were added around gym.

•1892•
North Star Creamery started.

Kenyon football team of 1909, pictured on south side of Forest Street grade and high school. Railroad tressel on right goes over Red Wing Ave. Most in the picture are unidentifiable, but front row, left to right, are: Carl Mogren, second row #5 Palmer Berg, top row, #2 Archie Kramer.

Kenyon High School basketball team of 1919. Front row, left to right: Herb Pattridge, Harold Rose, Ted Litsheim, Vernon Callister, Melvin Lips. Second row: James Sathrum, Walton Held, Ennert Borlaug. Top row unidentified.

•1981•

Parking on Main Street required to be parallel instead of angle parking.

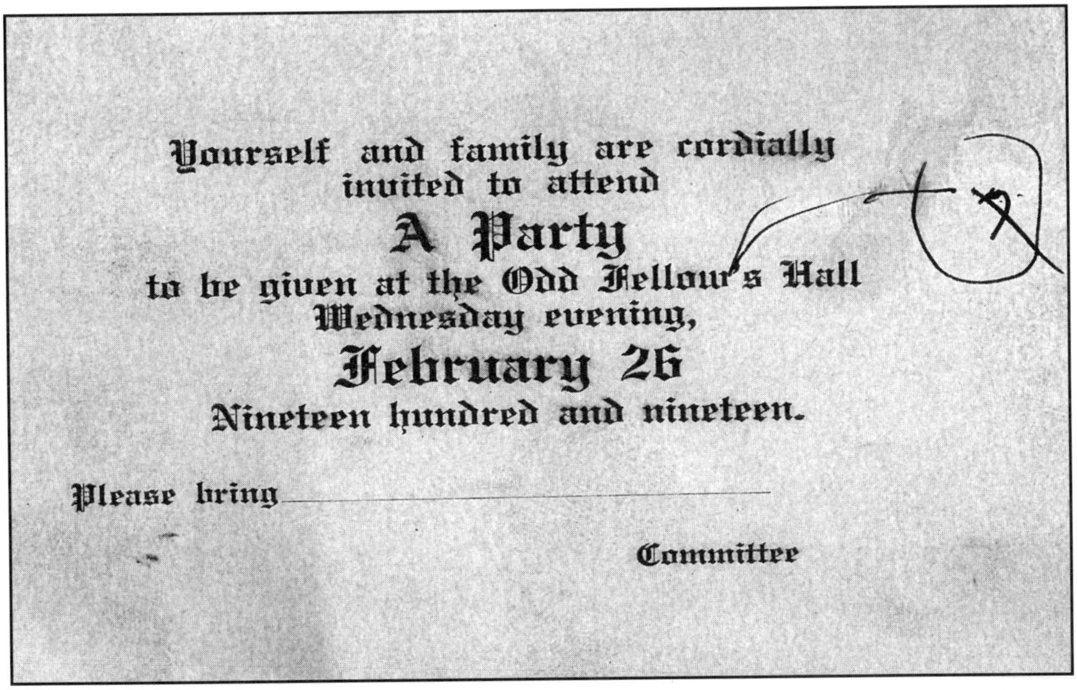

Yourself and family are cordially
invited to attend
A Party
to be given at the Odd Fellow's Hall
Wednesday evening,
February 26
Nineteen hundred and nineteen.

Please bring ____________________

Committee

This notice of a party at the Odd Fellows is printed on a two cent postal (during WWI postage was two cents and went back to one cent after war). My grandfather O.C. Cole made notation on card to remove apostrophe.

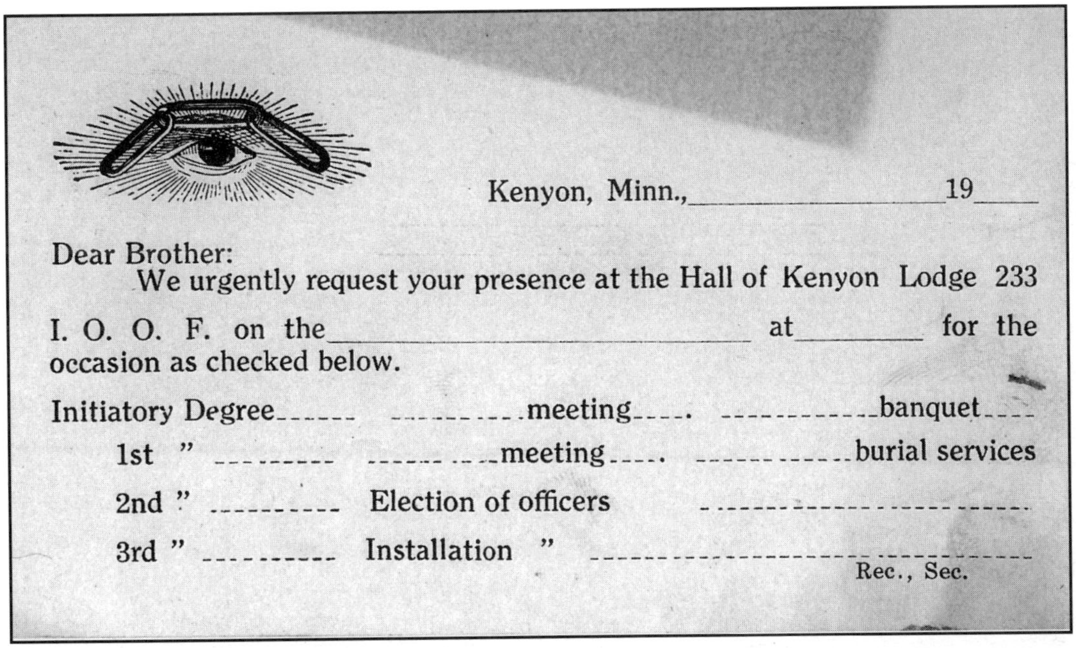

Kenyon, Minn.,_______________19____

Dear Brother:
We urgently request your presence at the Hall of Kenyon Lodge 233 I. O. O. F. on the____________________ at________ for the occasion as checked below.

Initiatory Degree______ __________meeting_____ ____________banquet____
1st " __________ __________meeting_____ ____________burial services
2nd " __________ Election of officers ____________
3rd " __________ Installation " ____________

Rec., Sec.

Most of the unused printed cards were found in a box that O.C. Cole kept of his printing from 1910 to 1920.

•1923•
Rum Runner from Faribault arrested in Kenyon with $400 worth of booze.

Another view of Milwaukee Railroad bridge east of Kenyon. Shadow of train running on Chicago Great Western track in lower view. Cement bridge pier still stands with date of 1903 marked on it. This is another set of cards put out by the Smiths Riceville, Iowa of which there are eight cards.

The picture on this post card was taken around 1918 as a two cent stamp was used on card. Motor Inn on left was selling Willis Knight and Overland cars. The Variety Store (which was Golden Rule) on right has lunch stand next to City Hall. The half-round hump in center of street says "Keep Right". From a set of at least eight cards by unknown maker.

•1948•
New sewer plant built on Pearl Creek and Highway 60.

Tressel looking from the east which is still standing. This picture was taken while under construction in 1903. Can you find the five workmen? *Post card by Robert Peterson.*

A westbound engine, tender, baggage car, and passenger car cross the long timber bridge over Pearl Creek. Circa 1910.

•1948•
Lagoon for Canning Co. waste built east of town.

The Chicago Milwaukee St. Paul Railroad Depot located in general area of present Linder-Villa apartments. Built in 1902 as combination depot and freight. Wood frame construction and measured 24' x 90'. Torn down in early 1960s.

Milwaukee train outside of Kenyon around 1914.

•1993•
Library moved and building razed to make room for new Coast to Coast store.

The Kenyon Milwaukee Depot by Austinson in early 1900s. Elevator in background belongs to L. Loomis. Sign to left of water tank says "Kenyon Lumber Co." The windmill is for filling water tank which in turn filled water tanks on steam trains.

Another view of Depot with train in front and one box car on side track. Circa 1909.

•1885•

Minnesota and Northwestern Railroad built track on long wood timber tressel over Zumbro River into Kenyon

J.T. Austinson photo of Milwaukee Train stuck in snow after trying to buck the large drifts. Circa 1910.

Another Austinson card post marked 1910. Milwaukee train with V Plow stuck in drift and had to be hand shoveled out.

•1926•
Community hall voted down.

Milwaukee Engine #1022 stuck in snow drift one mile west of Bombay March 15, 1951. *Post card by James Bjerkvig*

Milwaukee Engine #1037 has run V plow off track and trainmen are trying to put it back on. One mile west of Bombay April 21, 1951. *Post card by James Bjerkvig*

•1916•

The Metropolitan Club changed its name to Commercial Club.

This is the only card I cannot find. It should be of the Chicago Great Western Depot but so far it has eluded me. The Depot is still standing in Riverside Park next to the swimming pool.

The Chicago Great Western Depot built in 1885. It is a combination frame building (Depot and Freight) 22' x 70' long. Moved to city park in 1974 and now used as park shelter.

Looking north at Chicago Great Western rail yard. Elevator on left and Pearl Creek on right around 1910 era. Note two tracks, one main line on left and side track used by waiting trains on right.

•1945•
Kenyon Lions Club started.

This arrival card post marked 1907 let the address on the other side know that they got to Kenyon by using an "X" in the appropriate space.

Northbound Chicago Great Western train pulled by engine #77. Train crew standing in front probably waiting on side track for south bound train to pass. Taken in 1911.

•1961-62•
Kenyon Municipal Utilities paid regular customers November electric bills because of low expenses.

A Milwaukee west bound train, locomotive #133, tender and baggage car, passed over the Chicago Great Western tracks (main line and siding). Notice water tower for train in distance. Highway 56 is now located to left of bridge.

Chicago Great Western coal chute. Coal unloaded from railroad cars under shed was moved by steam hoppers up to bin in center of concrete tower. Steam trains needing coal would pull along side, lower chutes and coal would fill tender located behind engine. The chute was demolished in 1950s.

•1930•

Cooking school gives demonstration using a new development, Shellane bottled gas.

Another view of coal chute. Note right side of picture is a side car dump unloading facility and water tank on other side of Main Street. No written knowledge of the side dump facility can be found.

This 1909 card shows a rotary snow plow opening the deep cut one mile south of Kenyon on the Chicago Great Western tracks.

•1980•
First Carriage and Cutter Parade held in Kenyon.

Referred to as Church St as there were seven churches on Third Street. The church in background is the Baptist Church built in 1887. The steeple and east wing were taken off and building made into house. It's now 624-3rd St. owned by James Boden.

Standing on Red Wing Ave. looking west on Third St. Church in foreground is the German Methodist built around 1889. There is no record of what happened to the church but a house (222 Red Wing Ave.) stands there now. *Post card from Gladys Mund*

•1954•

The Kenyon Country Club installs first watering system on course.

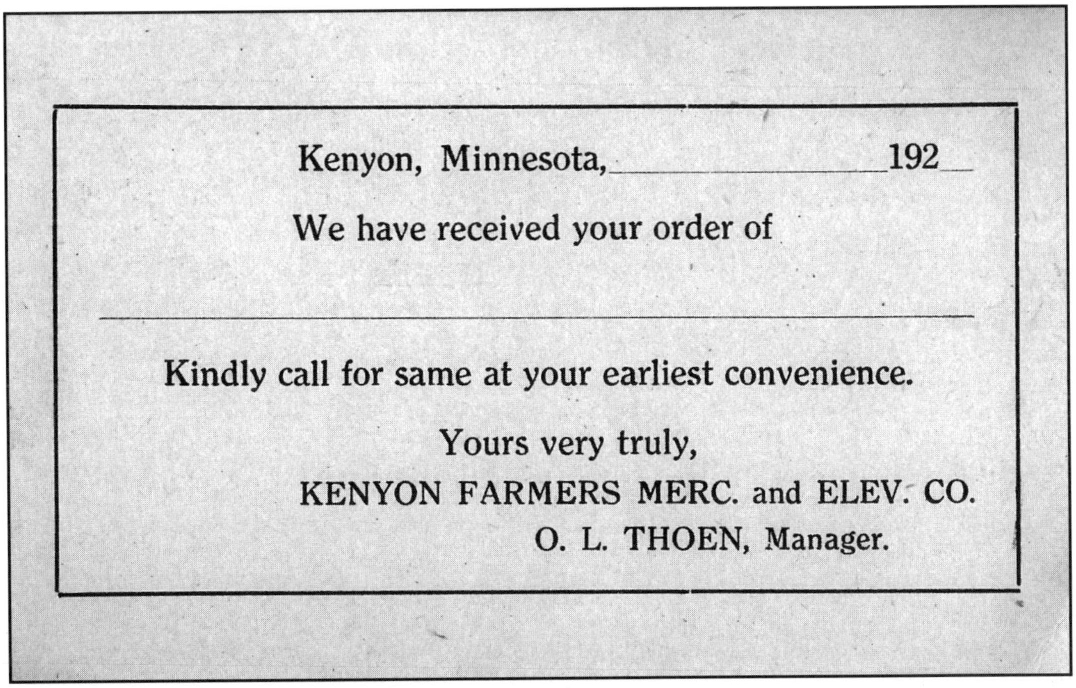

Kenyon, Minnesota,_______________192__

We have received your order of

____

Kindly call for same at your earliest convenience.

Yours very truly,

KENYON FARMERS MERC. and ELEV. CO.

O. L. THOEN, Manager.

As not all county residents had phones and those who did were on a party line, the use of post cards to notify a customer of the arrival of their order was very convenient.

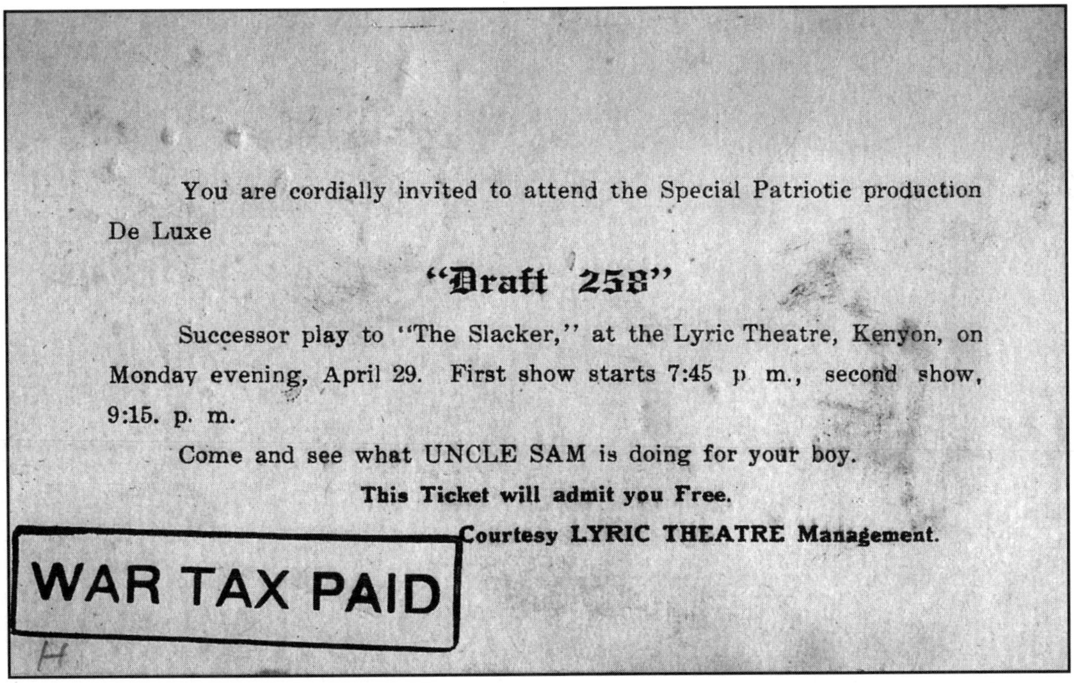

You are cordially invited to attend the Special Patriotic production De Luxe

"Draft 258"

Successor play to "The Slacker," at the Lyric Theatre, Kenyon, on Monday evening, April 29. First show starts 7:45 p. m., second show, 9:15. p. m.

Come and see what UNCLE SAM is doing for your boy.

This Ticket will admit you Free.

Courtesy LYRIC THEATRE Management.

WAR TAX PAID

H

This two cent postal was the ticket for a performance at the Lyric Theatre in 1918.

•1944•

"Club 21", a youth center, opened in the upstairs of the Clausen Opera House.

Some enterprising photographer may have gone through homes in Kenyon and photographed every house and had them put on post card paper. Above, house #70 is 419 Gunderson Boulevard owner Alice Held (Mrs. Frank Held and neighbor lady are pictured). Below, house #150 is 132 Second St. owner Oscar Munson (notice they left the outhouse door open).

•1902•

Rural free mail delivery started.

Homes on the boulevard in the early 1920s were, left to right: 315 Gunderson Boulevard - owner Joel Wrolstad; 309 Gunderson Boulevard - owner Elmer Underdahl; Empty lot - now home of Howard Held. Note street cleaner's cart to the right. *Post card by Gladys Mund*

The taking of pictures and having them put on post card paper was very common in the first 40 years of 1900. This way, relatives could get a picture of your home. This house was Christ Mund's that was demolished to make room for Fairway store on Red Wing Ave. *Post card by Gladys Mund*

•1958•

Part of Langford Avenue was closed for the North Star Creamery unloading building.

My great grandfather John Hansen built this home at 404 Forest St. It is the former Art Werdahl home now owned by Kevin Hildebrandt.

Around 1915, Pederson and Hilstad Hardware ran a special on Forman, Fords paint. Houses may look local but card was used by many dealers and supplied by paint company.

•1894•

Daily stage route for mail between Kenyon and Red Wing established.

A unique card. Small photos were glued to card. By changing picture, the card could be used by any town.

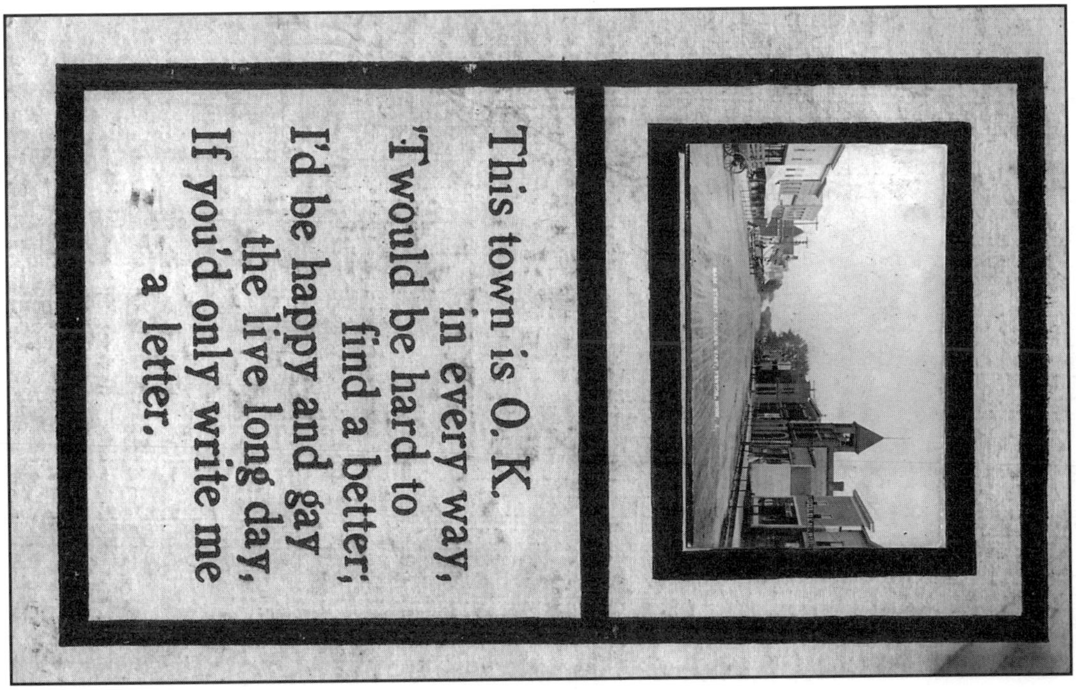

•1873•

A post card could be mailed for one cent until January 1952. In 1917 to 1919, the price raised to two cents but dropped back to a penny at the end of WWI.

Main Street in the early 1930s. New street lights have been installed. The metal rack on the trunk of the car on the right could be lowered so more suitcases could be tied on behind.

Late 1930s. Canopy on side of building on right covers stairway to Pool Hall located in basement. National Tea Grocery located one door east of Leutholds on left.

•1918•
On Nov. 11, Armistice Day, city hall and church bells rang for 16 hours.

This picture was taken around 1937. The Kenyon Co-op Oil Assn. was selling Globe gas. Note California style tile roof on station, also corn is growing in dirt opening by curb. Garage on left was the first Ford garage.

Kenyon's west-end city tourist park. Stone wall built around parking area by Civilian Conservation Corps (CCC). Bridge in background removed in 90s and river diverted to north side of Highway 60.

•1925•
Corn Show started as Market Day and Harvest Festival.

Burned in 1924 by a mysterious fire, this church was originally called First Norwegian Lutheran Church. Built in 1893 by J.L. Stene, a local contractor and builder, on the southeast corner of Forest and Third Street.

In 1925-26, a new brick church was constructed on the same spot. Note pile of sand for sidewalk and wood planks used as walkway into church.

•1962•
First year for the "Boulevard of Roses".

The First Evangelical Lutheran Church with pastor home on left. Home on right was moved to 418 Bullis St. in 1962 to make room for new addition to high school.

In 1962, a new education wing was added to the south side of the church to relieve crowded Sunday School space in church basement.

•1939•
The Kenyon Municipal Utilities Generating Plant was built.

The top card mailed in 1912 and the bottom card mailed in 1914 are examples of pennant cards. It was a card any town could use just by printing the town name in the flag area.

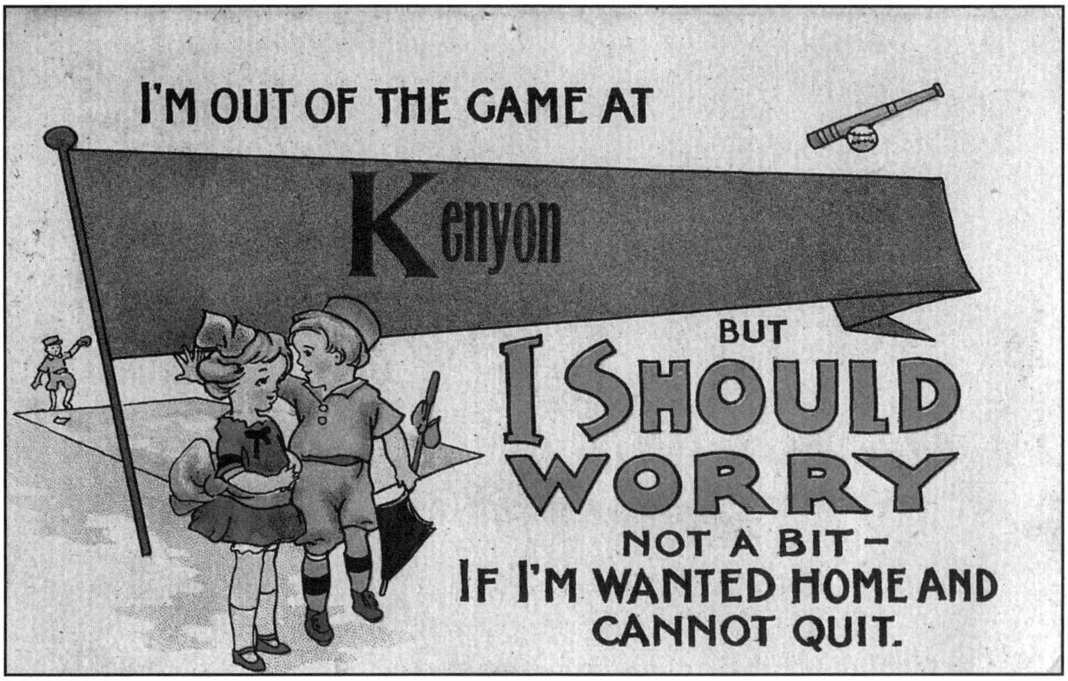

•1903•
First telephone directory released with 300 names.

Oscar Roise is selling Studebaker and Buick cars in the Hjermstad building in the 1940s.

Ray Burgess was owner of this new Kenyon Hotel and had a good trade from traveling salesmen. Rates were cheap, the place was clean and the bathroom was down the hall. Circa 1940s.

•1884•
Frank Held rode the first excursion train over the Chicago Great Western tracks in September.

North Star Creamery showing vacant lot between Kenyon Municipal Utilities generation building and main creamery plant. In 1945, a two story milk drying plant was built on this lot. Picture circa late 1930s.

Looking east toward the creamery in late 1940s showing the 128 foot smoke stack on the North Star Creamery. The stack was illuminated at night and commercial airlines would call when the light was out as it was used as a part of visual navigation. Creamery and stack were removed in 1995.

•1885•
American House by Depot was built by L.B. Slee.

Early 1940s. On the right, VFW is located upstairs. On left, Coast to Coast has moved next to Leutholds from a frame building just west of Held Chevrolet.

Late 1940 as utilities offices has been built and a milk drying addition has been added to the North Star Creamery.

•1903•
The east-west Milwaukee Railroad extended to Kenyon and Faribault from Zumbrota.

Early 1940s as Donald Stanton is selling Dodge and Plymouth cars in the Fox Garage on the left (fire hall). The wood frame building next to Smith's Garage on right is Zelners Meat Market.

A post card I had made prior to buildings being removed for new bank addition. Fairway building is empty.

•1998•
North Medical takes over operation of Kenyon Ambulance Service.

Corner of Main and Red Wing looking west in the early 1940s. The Time Theater is pictured on the left and Thune Theater is on the right (marquee just to left of highway sign). Best cowboy movies shown Friday and Saturday nights.

Main Street looking east from Spring Street in early 1940s. Kenyon Co-op Oil always had pretty flowers in space next to curb.

•1982•
The North-South Chicago and Northwestern Railroad tracks abandoned.

Looking east from Huseth Street in the early 1940s. Boulevard was Second Street then and only small bushes were growing there. Home on the left built by Dr. Fredric C. Meyer (132 Gunderson Blvd).

Looking west at an early view of the boulevard. Home on the left is the Raymond Gunderson home, now the Kenyon Sunset Home.

•1951•
Telephone company installs dial system.

The Kenyon Choral Union which appeared at the Nelson Opera Hall (located above VFW) is shown in costumes from "BELSHAZZAR" given April 24-26, 1912. Advertising on curtain above group says, "Henry Fladland for Furniture". Ole Steihaug is the photographer.

Kenyon Choral Union cast members of "Chimes of Normandy" on stage at Nelson Opera House in 1913. Guy on far left has long nose.

•1943•
Airport built just south of Kenyon along Highway 56.

One of Kenyon area churches. Built around 1877, this church is located one mile south of Skyberg on Highway 56. In 1894, a chancel and steeple were added. A new west entrance was built in 1968.

A multi-view of Kenyon churches, clockwise starting at 12 are: First Lutheran, German Evangelical, Hauge, Methodist.

•1940•
Ice skating rink opened on northeast corner of Spring and Sixth Street.

Moland Lutheran Church built in 1884. A parsonage was built on adjacent land in 1953.

This church, built in 1874 from stone cut from a quarry along the Zumbro River, is the oldest church in the area. In 1881, a parsonage was built across the road and in 1928 a guild hall was built west of the church. In 1976, a new parish hall was built along with a new entrance to the church.

•1907•

Santino's Military Band appeared at the Nelson Opera House.

The Kenyon Municipal Swimming Pool was constructed in 1955 for $80,000 by a vote of city residents. My daughters Lynn, Wendy, and Sherry are in this photo.

The Martin T. Gunderson House given to the people of Kenyon in 1975. M.T. had P.L. Kramer build this house in 1895 for his family who lived here until Hattie died. The home is listed on the National Register of Historic Places and operates as a local attraction by the Kenyon Historical Society.

•1892

The Minnesota and Northwestern Railroads were taken over by the Chicago Great Western Railroad and they ran it for the next 66 years.

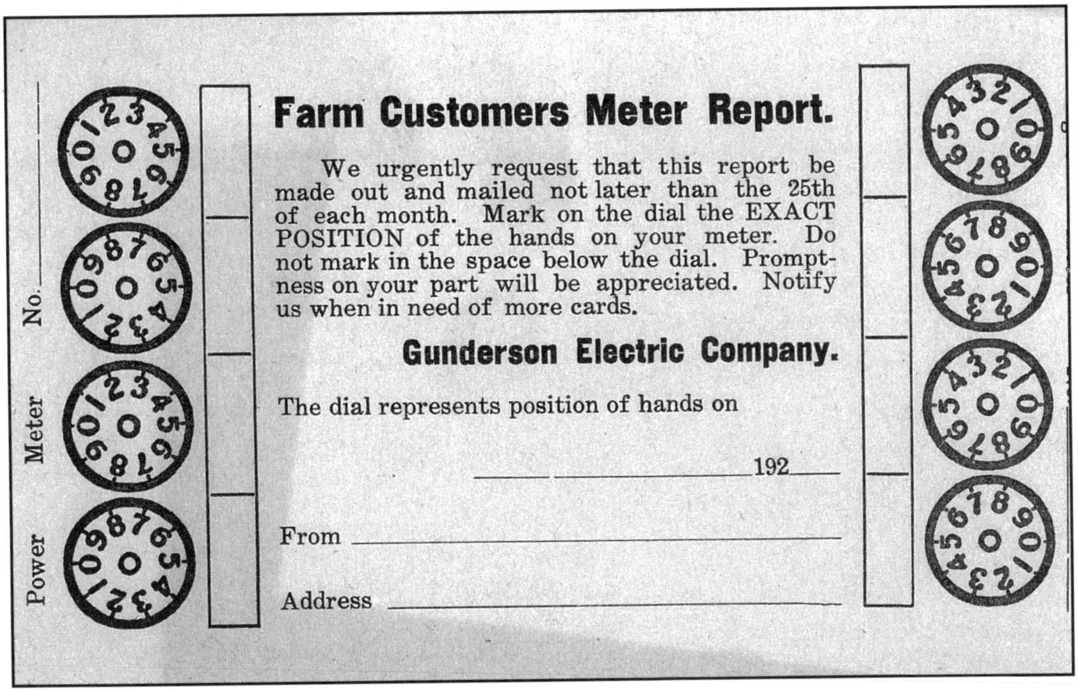

Farm Customers Meter Report.

We urgently request that this report be made out and mailed not later than the 25th of each month. Mark on the dial the EXACT POSITION of the hands on your meter. Do not mark in the space below the dial. Promptness on your part will be appreciated. Notify us when in need of more cards.

Gunderson Electric Company.

The dial represents position of hands on

________________192____

From ______________________________

Address ______________________________

Power Meter No. ______________

This penny postal was used for reading electric meters of a homeowner. Every month a mark would be made on the card where the arrow was pointing on the four dials of the meter. For the cost of a penny postal, Gunderson could have all the meters recorded at a small cost to the electric company.

Canning Season - - Now on

PEACHES--Fancy Elberta's per crate	$1.45
COLD-PACK Jar rings . .	10c
PAROWAX per pound . .	16c
JAR CAPS--Best grade per dozen .	35c

There are several grades of peaches on the market--we have the best--you should can this week on account of the railroad strike pending.

Dowling's Cash Store

Notice of peaches arriving at the grocery store is not such a big thing as it was years ago. Home canned products kept many families supplied with fruits and vegetables through the long winter months. E.D. Dowling ran a store from 1917 to 1922 at 637 2nd. St.

•1949•

Boy Scouts had a cabin with stone fireplace in Elcock park

The original Country Club house. Man standing on porch is George Hanson, local funeral director, and Howard Klug (standing by tree), owner of a motion picture theater. Post marked 1945.

Picture looking at Country Club house from the west parking lot. Circa 1960s.

•1976•
Last Milwaukee train to run on 35 miles of track from Zumbrota to Faribault.

Looking at #9 green from the Club house. Only pull carts were allowed at this time. Circa 1960s.

In the 1970s, an addition was added to the south complete with a deck. A locker room and larger kitchen facilities made it a great improvement.

•1948•
Kenyon purchases first police patrol car.

This team must be going or coming from a parade. The owner of this rig was so proud of it that he had post cards made to send to his friends. Taken at the corner of Huseth and Gunderson Boulevard. House on right is 100 Gunderson Blvd. now owned by John Davidson, Jr.

This card sent out by Lampert's Lumber Yard introduces everyone to Con Stucky, new manager of the Lumber Yard 1954-56.

•1968•

The Chicago Great Western Railroad taken over by the Chicago and Northwestern Railroad and they ran it for the next 14 years.

These are wallpaper cards. A.P. Brobeck Drug Store sold wall covering and these cards were supposed to let you know new lines were in. Post marked 1909.

•1917•
Sommers Cannon Co. purchased Kenyon Canning Co.

The Mahlon Bullis home built in 1904 was the first Catholic Church (St. Michaels) to locate in Kenyon in 1943. This house was later moved to 501 Forest St. where it is used as a residence.

The new St. Michael Church built in 1955 was dedicated by Archbishop John Gregory Murry. The former church can be seen in background.

•1961•

Pipe line installed and natural gas comes to Kenyon.

St. Michaels Church to the right adds to the beauty of Kenyon's boulevard.

Another view of St. Michaels just after it was built. In 1986, a parish center and parking lot was constructed on the rear of the church.

•1940•
Last year for very popular "Corn Show"

Looking east on Main just about noon in the 1960s. Pure gasoline is selling for 27.9 cents. New fluorescent street lights have been installed.

A busy day in town in the early 1960s. Bowling pin sign on left in front of Bowlitorium. Clark Hardware is on the right.

•1896•

M.T. Gunderson installed first electric generator.

Main and Red Wing in the early 1960s. Standard is selling gas for 27.9 cents. KMU old line truck parked in front of utilities. One of the first riding lawn mowers on display outside Implement building.

Post marked 1963. Liquor Store next to Jorstad Hardware stands empty on right. One left, Old Time Theatre marquee painted with lounge as it is new home of Municipal Liquor Store.

•1922•
Lutefisk suppers were priced at 25 cents.

Boulevard of Roses. In 1962, multi-colored tree roses were planted. Over the years, they have been a delight to see by local residents as well as those passing through our community. House on the right is 304 Gunderson Blvd.

Boulevard of Roses in the 1960s still called Second Street. It wasn't changed to Gunderson Blvd. until 1975. Homes on the left are 315, 309, and 303 Gunderson Blvd.

•1884•
Kenyon businesses gave $15,000 to locate the Minnesota and Northwestern Railroad tracks through Kenyon.

An early spring day in 1973 on Main Street. Mike Wunderlich has his bedding plants on the sidewalk in front of his grocery store on the right.

Note stately Elm trees which once lined the boulevard like a large umbrella. Circa early 1960s. Jon Held just left his bicycle in front of his parent's home (304 Gunderson Boulevard) and is going to talk to the caretaker mowing grass at the Byron Gunderson Home (222 Gunderson Blvd.). Jon now lives in Byron's home.

•1959•
Mobile home park started with five lots.

This photo of Holden Church just after it was built in 1924. The Holden congregation dates back to 1856.

Looking north through the main gates of church property with lime rock wall on south edge of cemetery.

•1935•

Active fraternal groups were VFW, American Legion, A.F. and A.M., O.E.S., I.O.O.F., O. of B., A.O.U.W., M.W.A., D.O.F.O., Round Table Club, Literary Guild, Isaac Walton League, and P.T.A.

A view of Holden Church with iron fence which replaced lime rock wall.

This church replaces the first Dale Church built in 1877 which was destroyed by fire in 1947. The stone wall on the north of the church was built in 1924.

•1948•
"Pop" Hamann distributed his carbonated soft drink "Silver Sparkles".

These two cards bring Minnesota into play as the 1920 card uses the state seal and the 1940 card has the state capitol and state flower plus views of Minnesota in the word Minnesota.

•1974•
Kenyon officially changed from Village to City.

The purchase of the Raymond T. Gunderson home on the boulevard in 1949 gave Kenyon its first large senior care facility. The garage at left was converted into housing for residents. The house far left was purchased in 1953 for housing administrator.

The Sunset Home has been added to over the years and this is what it looked like in the 1970s.

•1949•
The Kenyon Sunset Home had its first resident.

– Your Personal Postcards –

JOHN COLE – PUBLIC SERVANT, HISTORIAN!!

John Cole has been a public servant in the City of Kenyon most of his adult life, having served as a member of the City Council for a number of years, and three different stints as mayor of the community. His role in local government totaled more than 16 years, and ended in 1994 when he chose not to seek re-election.

His service to his community did not end at that time, however. He and his wife, Lila, have been long-time board members and active contributors to the American Red Cross Chapter in Goodhue County, and he currently serves as a member of the Goodhue County Historical Society. John also serves as a commissioner from Goodhue County on the Southeastern Minnesota Multi-County Housing and Redevelopment Authority. He also is an active member of the Kenyon Lions Club.

John's interest in history and penchant for 'collecting' led him to a hobby that will help preserve Kenyon's past for generations to come. He discovered there is amazing history recorded in postcards, and he has devoted countless hours and effort in building a collection to help capsule the history of this community and area.

Cole started his collection in 1974 and recently counted more than 5,000 post cards in his possession. He and Lila attend special 'card' shows, visit antique dealers anywhere they can find them, and are at countless auctions. He always hopes to pick up that special card to add to his history. He continually buys and trades for cards, and friends and area residents who recognize the historical significance of his collection often give him prized cards they feel need to be preserved.

John has now chosen to share some of that history by publishing this book, and preserving forever a part of the record he has accumulated. There are some 212 cards printed here, and Cole identifies and gives a background for each picture. For those natives of the area, the book will help document some of the historical data they lived as children and young adults; for those of us who are relative newcomers it will help explain the proud tradition of Kenyon and its residents.

Robert Stumm, a free-lance writer and past president of the Twin Cities Postcard Club, has stated: "So much can be learned from postcards — they really can be the picture worth a 1,000 words."

John Cole deserves a pat on the back for his collection, and helping preserve and document Kenyon's rich history through his post cards. Some day the complete collection will find a significant home where it will become a permanent historical document. Until then you'll want his book!

Robert D. (Bob) Noah
Kenyon Leader Publisher